RENEWED RECOVERY

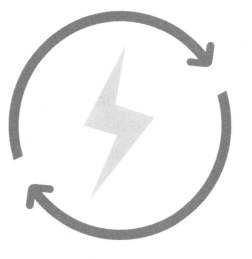

Breakup Workbook for Christians - Healing and Restoration Guide to thrive after the Breakup.

God's Hand Publishers

About the Author

We're glad you're here at God's Hand Publishers, a place where we produce Christian-based workbooks that help adults, kids and teenagers. At God's Hand Publishers, we have a strong conviction in the influence of faith and how it may change a person's life.

John Raymond, the founder of our organization and primary writer, is a fervent supporter of mental wellness and enlightenment. John Raymond set out on a mission to develop materials that would encourage people to view life's challenges through the prism of faith because he had a strong desire to serve God and be of service to others.

John Raymond has a background in religion and psychology. We consider it a privilege to collaborate with people, congregations, institutions of higher learning, and other groups who value spiritual development and mental health. Let's go on a spiritually-based journey of self-discovery together as we face the difficulties of life and develop into the unique people God created us to be.

Thank you for joining us on this transformative path. May God's hand guide you every step of the way, in **faith and service,**

God's Hand Publishers

OTHER WORKBOOKS FROM THIS AUTHOR

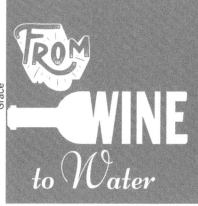

Finding Freedom Through Faith and Grace

ALCOHOL ADDICTION RECOVERY WORKBOOK FOR CHRISTRIANS

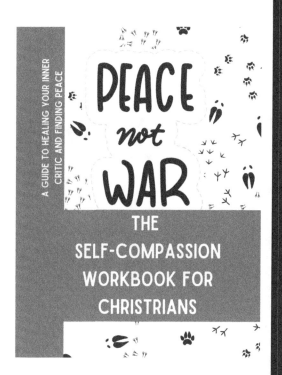

A GUIDE TO HEALING YOUR INNER CRITIC AND FINDING PEACE

THE SELF-COMPASSION WORKBOOK FOR CHRISTIANS

TABLE
OF CONTENTS

01 BALANCE

02 GRIEVE

03 ACCEPTANCE

04 FORGIVENESS

05 CAGE THE PAST

06 IDENTITY RENEWAL

07 SELF-ESTEEM

08 SOLO GOALS

09 SUPPORT CIRCLE

10 PATIENCE

INTRODUCTION

Movies make it seem so easy to get over a breakup. After a bad breakup, the individual simply goes home, puts on some pajamas, sobs while binge-watching a movie, goes on Spotify, and plays more sad songs, before you know it boom!!! they are back to the gym and hanging out with friends.

I wish it was that easy to get over, I wish my own breakup didn't almost paralyze my business. When you hit rock bottom after a breakup it affects everything, from the plans you both made together, the dreams of having kids, traveling around the world, all of that turns into a mere mist.

One thing saved me, and that thing is the word of God, It made me realize my life's purpose is much bigger than just a relationship, no one should have that much power over your emotions and feelings. Courtship before marriage as Christians is important in this day and time but it is much difficult to find someone who is equally yoked.

This workbook was born out of my personal experience as an individual, a counselor, and most importantly a child of God. I have spent many years helping individuals going through a bad breakup. The pages hold activities and exercises that will guide you wholly on your recovery.

Healing takes time, the activities in this workbook can take you weeks, months, or even a year to go through but be patient. Patience is one of the fruits of the spirit, I know it's hard but I know God heals the brokenhearted, so I say welcome to your healing destination.

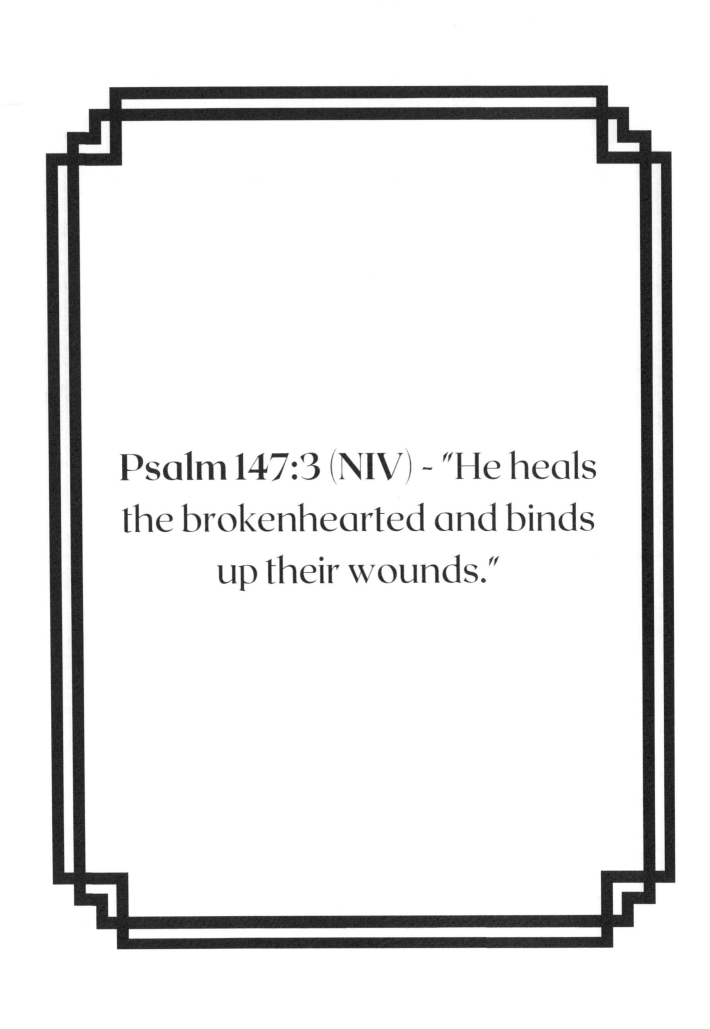

Psalm 147:3 (NIV) - "He heals the brokenhearted and binds up their wounds."

BALANCE

Psalm 55:22 (NIV) - *"Cast your cares on the Lord and he will sustain you; he will never let the righteous be shaken."*

One of the most difficult experiences I've ever had was a breakup I went through a few years ago. I experienced a complete sense of disorientation. I felt frustrated, upset, and perplexed. I wasn't sure how I was going to proceed.

It may be extremely challenging and traumatic to end a relationship. Managing the emotional swings of loss, rage, despair, and loneliness can be challenging. Getting used to life without your ex-partner can sometimes be difficult.

Proverbs 3:5-6 (NIV) reminds us, "Trust in the Lord with all your heart and lean not on your own understanding; in all your ways submit to him, and he will make your paths straight." During a breakup, our own understanding often feels insufficient, and that's when we need to lean on God's wisdom.

It takes giving up control and trusting God's divine plan to find balance and peace in such chaotic times. We must never forget that He has a bigger plan for our lives than just one particular relationship.

Finding balance and peace in the middle of the emotional turbulence that follows a breakup is not just a luxury; it is a crucial requirement.

As Christians, we draw strength from our faith to navigate the stormy seas of heartbreak and find solace in the arms of God. This journey toward balance and calm is not only essential for our emotional well-being but is also deeply intertwined with our spiritual growth.

Below are suggested faith-based activities you can engage in to find balance and calm during a breakup. Remember a troubled mind can't hear from God or make wise decisions.

Activity	Description	Scripture
Pray	Tell God how you're feeling and ask for His support and direction.	**Psalm 34:18** "The Lord is close to the brokenhearted and saves those who are crushed in spirit."
Read the Bible	Look for verses that uplift you and serve as a reminder of God's love.	**Romans 8:28** "And we know that in all things God works for the good of those who love him, who have been called according to his purpose."
Attend church or other religious services	Surround yourself with other Christians who can provide assistance and inspiration.	**Hebrews 10:25** "Let us not give up meeting together, as some are in the habit of doing, but let us encourage one another—and all the more as you see the Day approaching."
Fasting and Prayer	Think about using fasting as a spiritual practice, along with intense prayer, to find strength and clarity.	**Joel 2:12 (NIV)** "Even now," declares the LORD, "return to me with all your heart, with fasting and weeping and mourning."

Activity	Description	Scripture
Sing worship songs	Listen to Christian worship music that encourages you and brings you closer to God.	**Psalm 96:1** "Oh come, let us sing to the Lord; let us shout for joy to the Rock of our salvation."
Retreats and Pilgrimages	To strengthen your spiritual connection and find comfort, organize a retreat or pilgrimage to a holy location.	**Psalm 42:1-2 (NIV)** "As the deer pants for streams of water, so my soul pants for you, my God. My soul thirsts for God, for the living God. When can I go and meet with God?"
Do something kind for someone else	This might assist you in shifting your attention away from your problems and onto those of others.	**Galatians 6:2** "Carry each other's burdens, and in this way you will fulfill the law of Christ." drive_spreadsheetExport to Sheets

EXERCISE

During a breakup it's hard to gather our thought process, that's why it's always recommended to find some ounce of balance or calm so that you can truly know exactly what's happening.

Whether you are breaking up with your partner or the other way round, there must be tangible reasons for this action, as you can't just "un-love," someone you once loved.

The exercise below is tagged "what happened," These are vital questions you need to ask yourself before proceeding to the next chapter. Be sincere and precise with the answers as this will give a clear view of what's truly going on. You may now engage.

What happened?

How did the relationship end?

Who ended the relationship?

Why did the relationship end?

Is there room for reconciliation?

PROMPTS

Do you believe that God has a plan for your life, even in the midst of this difficult time?

_____

_____

_____

How can you draw on your faith to find hope and strength?

_____

_____

_____

_____

PRAYER

Dear Heavenly Father,

I come to you with heartache, a loss, and deep pain, I seek your grace and strength to find balance in my shaky moment. You are God and it is written that you will never leave me nor abandon me. Grant me balance.

In Jesus's name, Amen.

BIBLE MEDITATTION

These passages serve as a reminder of God's support, presence, and direction in the midst of heartache and turmoil. Think on these Bible scriptures.

Proverbs 3:5-6 (NIV): *"Trust in the Lord with all your heart and lean not on your own understanding; in all your ways submit to him, and he will make your paths straight."*

Romans 8:28 (NIV): *"And we know that in all things God works for the good of those who love him, who have been called according to his purpose."*

② GRIEVE

Matthew 5:4 (NIV) - *"Blessed are those who mourn, for they will be comforted."*

A few nights after my breakup, I remember waking up in the middle of the night, and I felt a strong pain in my heart, It was so deep that I couldn't hold back the tears. It was as if something had hurt me physically but it was all emotional.

You can't suppress the pain that comes from a broken relationship, it's like desiring to sail but saying you don't need the ocean for this to happen.

Let the pain hit you hard and feel every ounce of it through your bones but hold on to the altar of God because that is where genuine comfort comes from.

Cry!!! don't hold back the tears. Crying is not a sign of weakness but it takes genuine and authentic strength to let out those emotions.

Think about your breakup as a physical injury, that is meant to hurt and you're allowed to feel the pain.

There's no healing without pain or loss, the breakup is the injury and God is your healer, it will be hard to get healed if we fail to surrender to this hurt.

I know sometimes people think it is weak to show emotions because of a relationship that ended, but that is all a fallacy. You are human and God created you to feel emotions and you shouldn't hide that part of you.

I recall days when I locked myself in my bedroom, binge-watching movies and crying by myself, or when I was at my workplace, I would shut my door and just cry for some time, this helped me heal fast, and feeling these emotions helped me grow stronger.

I have encountered individuals who come up to me and tell me they felt weak for crying over a breakup and I reassured them that is completely natural for this to happen.

Matthew 5:4 (NIV) "Blessed are those who mourn, for they will be comforted," This verse assures us that when we mourn, the holy spirit is readily available to comfort us as long as we open ourselves to receive him.

EXERCISE

There are several emotions you will feel when you choose to finally grieve, but the main focus of this exercise is to truly allow yourself to be buried in these emotions. Skipping this part always comes back to hunt those that do it.

You can't numb yourself out with work, or events. This journey of grieving is meant for you to go through gracefully.

Below is a list of several emotions you are meant to feel after a breakup. Circle the actual ones you are currently feeling. Afterwards look at the table below and you will find suggested ways to express these emotions.

If the emotion you're currently feeling is not listed out on the diagram above, write it out here yourself.

Emotion	Expression
Sadness	When you feel like crying, allow yourself to. It can be a therapeutic discharge of suppressed feelings.
Anger	To relieve tension, engage in physical activities like yoga, boxing, or running.
Regret	Think about the relationship's lessons learnt and how you may use them in the future.
Loneliness	For company and support, get in touch with friends and family.

Emotion	Expression
Anxiety	When you're feeling worried, practicing deep breathing might assist your nervous system relax.
Confusion	To clarify your misunderstanding on paper, jot down your ideas and inquiries.
Numbness	To reestablish a connection with your body, engage in sensory activities like a warm bath or a massage.
Shame	Apply self-compassion by treating oneself with the same courtesy and consideration that you would extend to a friend in a comparable circumstance.

PROMPTS

Which big emotions are you constantly feeling and how are you expressing it?

_____

_____

_____

How does it feel to let out these emotions?

_____

_____

_____

_____

PRAYER

Dear Heavenly Father,

I thank you for your care and understanding as my heart continues to ache, give me the power to go through this grieving period as I understand that Joy comes in the morning.

In Jesus's name, Amen.

BIBLE MEDITATTION

These passages remind us that while it is normal to experience grief in the face of loss and difficulties, as Christians we may rely on our trust in God for strength, consolation, and the knowledge that He will be by our sides in all our troubles.

Psalm 30:5 (NIV)*: "For his anger lasts only a moment, but his favor lasts a lifetime; weeping may stay for the night, but rejoicing comes in the morning."*

John 16:22 (NIV)*: "So with you: Now is your time of grief, but I will see you again and you will rejoice, and no one will take away your joy."*

3 ACCEPTANCE

After grieving the loss of this connection, acceptance becomes simpler, just as the sun appears after rain. There are no more tears in you since you have already sobbed them all out. At this time, even though you may still mourn them, you have accepted your split and are prepared to move on.

The 'acceptance' stage focuses mostly on assimilating loss and making it a part of your experience. It's about gaining knowledge that will enable you to steer clear of repeating the same errors and unhealthy relationship practices.

Life will get simpler from now on as long as you remain loyal to yourself and never lose focus on your emotional requirements.

You've been able to find peace with the end of the relationship, the loss of their affection, and the sense of security you shared.

Additionally, you gave up on the imagined, idealized future in which you and your ex would spend the rest of your time together.

Your outlook on life has improved, and you've effectively applied the lessons you've taken away from this bad event.

The animosity you've had toward your ex could disappear depending on your personality, character, and other variables that you may or may not be aware of. This makes room for a sober assessment of all that has transpired between you two, one that is reasonable and maybe even sympathetic.

However, there is always a chance that you will feel regret, anger, or guilt, but eventually you will come to terms with the situation as it is.

You'll eventually come to the realization that your relationship has ended, your ex is no longer a part of your life, and you have every reason to go on and start over. But this time, you'll be more capable, knowledgeable, and self-assured.

Remember that without all the bad feelings you had to experience, acceptance would not have been possible.

Therefore, allow yourself to have a terrible day, weep, or momentarily distance yourself from daily concerns.

Although you could feel a variety of emotions throughout the "acceptance" stage, what matters most is that you no longer desire to continue the connection.

Remember In Psalm 55:22 - "Cast your cares on the Lord, and he will sustain you." This passage teaches us to lay down the broken-heartedness and see the wonderful working power of Christ Jesus.

EXERCISE

If you were the one who got broken up with, it could take you a little longer to comprehend what has occurred. However, choosing to terminate a relationship is not something that is simple for anyone to do.

The first step to acceptance is trying to write out everything you both planned you were going to do in the future, whether it was buying a home together, going to that dream holiday destination, or having those babies within a year of marriage.

Write it on the cloud below, then completely shade it off. You can also write it on another piece of paper, completely shred it, flush it, or burn it in a safe space. This ritual comes with you accepting that there is no tomorrow between you two.

PROMPTS

How do you feel during this acceptance stage?

_____

_____

_____

Is there anything that's holding you back from accepting the end of this relationship and why?

_____

_____

_____

PRAYER

Dear Heavenly Father,

Thank you for bringing me to this phase of acceptance, I have come to realize that you are my refuge and strength. Teach me to let go and accept the things I can't change.

In Jesus's name, Amen.

BIBLE MEDITATTION

These passages stress the necessity of having confidence, trust, and hope in God amid trying times with the knowledge that He is by our sides and is able to make a difference in our lives.

__Psalm 46:1-2 (NIV)__ - "God is our refuge and strength, an ever-present help in trouble. Therefore we will not fear, though the earth give way and the mountains fall into the heart of the sea."

__Jeremiah 29:11 (NIV)__ - "For I know the plans I have for you," declares the Lord, "plans to prosper you and not to harm you, plans to give you hope and a future."

FORGIVENESS

After a breakup, forgiveness can be extremely difficult. In many circumstances, our partner's actions wounded us before the actual split; in fact, the hurt's accumulation is frequently what led to the breakup in the first place.

When a relationship ends, we frequently feel betrayed, humiliated, abandoned, shamed, embarrassed, and harmed all over. Sometimes we may look back and identify a specific cause for this, but other times we are simply left wondering why we have gone through such suffering.

If you were mistreated in a previous relationship, you might be inclined to exact revenge by criticizing your ex or trying to sabotage your next relationship.

But it's crucial to take the right course of action. If not for your ex, then at least for yourself, choose peace and forgiveness.

Holding a grudge is burdensome and it can hold you back from truly letting go. *It is written in Ephesians 4:31-32 (NIV) -"Get rid of all bitterness, rage and anger, brawling and slander, along with every form of malice. Be kind and compassionate to one another, forgiving each other, just as in Christ God forgave you."*

You need to let go and forgive in order to be completely free. If necessary, this may require you to entirely cut off contact with your ex. God's purpose is much bigger than anything you can accomplish on your own. You may put your confidence in the fact that God has a greater plan for your life if a relationship doesn't work out.

If you give your heart to God, you may be assured that something better is waiting for you in the future than your former connection.

It can be difficult to move on from a prior relationship, especially if you believed they were "the one." You must have faith in God at these times. Even if it might not make sense, if you follow the Lord, you'll always end up where you need to be and with the perfect person.

EXERCISE

Our emotions sometimes become entangled with forgiveness, which causes us to complicate it. What if I told you, "Forgiveness isn't complicated, but it is difficult."

Forgiveness is a verb, which means it is an action. It is referred to as debt cancellation. It is a deliberate decision we make to erase someone else's debt. In order to do this, we pardon them (Romans 12:17-19). To put it another way, forgiveness is achieved by giving the issue to God.

We want forgiveness to be an emotion or feeling rather than an action, which creates confusion about what forgiveness is. The harm or damage that has been caused cannot be undone by pardoning the offender.

Simply put, choosing to forgive is the first act of submission to God. Additionally, this will serve as the start of the healing process. You will most surely be prevented from starting the healing process if you refuse to forgive.

Write out a list of grudges you are still holding against your ex-partner on the notepad below. Then use the diagram beneath as a symbol of forgiveness by writing within it. Starting each phrase with the word "I forgive," e.g. "I forgive you for……"

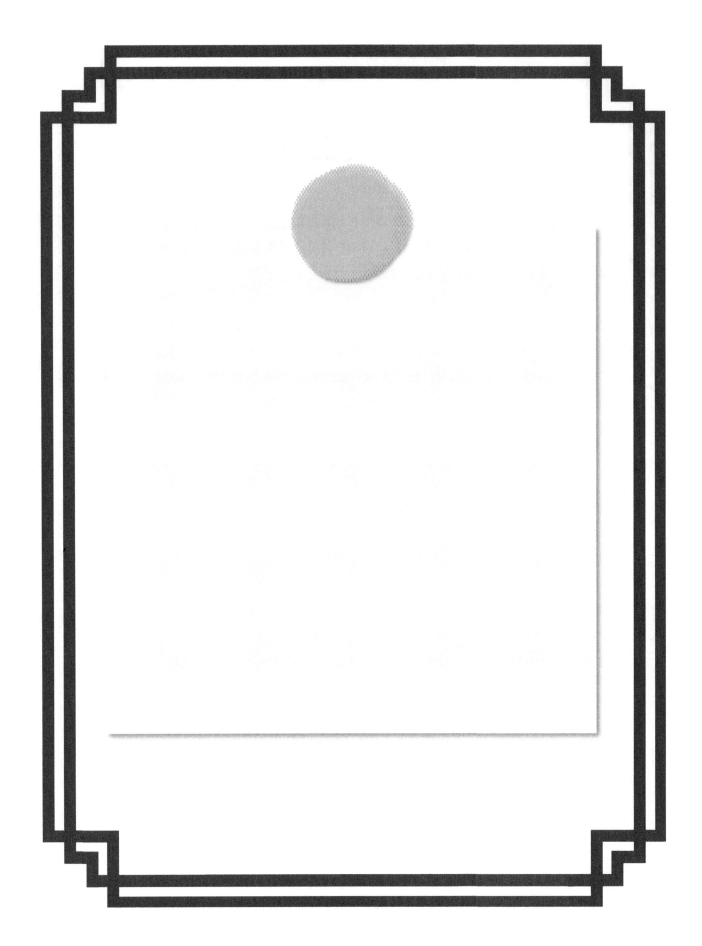

I forgive you for

PROMPTS

What does forgiveness mean to you?

How does it feel to truly forgive?

PRAYER

Dear Heavenly Father,

I thank you for forgiving me for my trespasses as I have chosen to forgive those who have trespassed against me. Give me the divine grace to forgive and let go.

In Jesus's name, Amen.

BIBLE MEDITATTION

It might be challenging to get past a previous relationship. But it's crucial to take stock of both the good and the bad in order to heal, grow, and move on. The verses below will assist you in doing exactly that.

Psalm 34:17-18 - *"The righteous cry out, and the Lord hears them; he delivers them from all their troubles. The Lord is close to the brokenhearted and saves those who are crushed in spirit."*

Psalm 73:26 - *"My flesh and my heart may fail, but God is the strength of my heart and my portion forever."*

5 CAGE THE PAST

Ecclesiastes 3:1 (NIV) -*"There is a time for everything and a season for every activity under the heavens."*

Physically letting someone leave is different than psychologically letting them go after forgiveness. Caging the past involves getting rid of any objects or places that serve as unpleasant triggers.

If a particular restaurant reminds you of them and this makes you sad, why don't you try a whole different restaurant?

Maybe it's a T-shirt you both had, it is time to place it inside a box, either give it back to them or donate it to a shelter.

If you both share a Netflix account, or there's anything that brings back all these memories that make you feel sad, you should cage it all up in a box and let it go.

This is not about erasing them from your life, it's simply you trying to build a new identity for yourself that doesn't involve them in any way.

Isaiah 43:18-19 (NIV) "Forget the former things; do not dwell on the past. See, I am doing a new thing! Now it springs up; do you not perceive it? I am making a way in the wilderness and streams in the wasteland." This verse clearly informs us that it is okay to forget the old things and not dwell on them for what is coming will make it worth it.

As I clearly stated in the previous chapter, maybe you will have to block them on social media, I know it's hard not to look up what they are currently doing or who they are hanging out with, but believe me from experience this will only weaken your recovery phase.

EXERCISE

Even while you might think that speaking with or seeing your ex lover will bring about closure, staying in touch usually just makes the pain last longer.

It's crucial to break digital links, too. How significant? According to one study, those who digitally stalk their ex-partners are less happy, store more unfavorable emotions, experience more desire, and limit their ability to grow personally more than those who break social media links.

Below is a box; fill it with anything you need to throw away or replace in order to box the past and let it go. Write it down and design it.

PROMPTS

How difficult was this actual exercise?

How do you feel about caging the past?

PRAYER

Dear Heavenly Father,

I thank you for being with me through this process of grieving and recovery from a broken relationship. Grant me the boldness to cage my past and accept the future you have set out for me.

In Jesus's name, Amen.

BIBLE MEDITATTION

Meditate on these Bible verses as you seek for strength to truly let go of the past and move on with the future God has set out for you.

Proverbs 4:23 (NIV) - *"Above all else, guard your heart, for everything you do flows from it."*

2 Corinthians 5:17 (NIV) - *"Therefore, if anyone is in Christ, the new creation has come: The old has gone, the new is here!"*

6 IDENTITY RENEWAL

Ephesians 1:5 *"He predestined us for adoption to sonship through Jesus Christ, in accordance with his pleasure and will."*

I can still picture myself stepping outdoors in the snow after my passionate relationships ended and gazing up at the gloomy dark sky. Why, I kept asking God. I almost gasped for air when I heard the response, but I had to smile.

God said, "Because I am jealous for you."

That is the thing about walking with Jesus. Either you're all in or all out. He doesn't want half-hearted disciples who would probably compromise their beliefs.

My ability to develop into the Christian I was meant to be was hindered by that previous relationship. Nobody was at fault; it was just not meant to be.

At first, you might feel a little adrift if you and your ex do decide to split up. When a habit breaks, it almost feels as though you have lost some of who you are since your ideas and lifestyle habits have been in unionism with another person through the years.

It's time to turn to a new page with open arms and self-discovery when that chapter of your life comes to an end. Although it won't be simple and may take some time, there is a far larger reason why you must do this.

It may be simple to lose oneself in a lifestyle and forget who one was as a person when someone has been in a relationship for the most of their life.

It's time to start focusing on the good things in life right now. While it's normal to require time to get over your loss and grieve, it is also the ideal moment to rediscover who you are and choose exactly what you want from life.

EXERCISE

The next set of exercises is to reconnect you with your identity. We tend to forget ourselves when we get into a long relationship, I'm talking about remembering our likes and dislikes, what we enjoy doing, and so on.

This is completely natural as humans but I want you to discover who you were before the relationship and who you've grown to become.

The first activity requires you to write an autobiography about yourself that accurately describes who you are. The second exercise requires you to spend the following five days taking at least five minutes each day to pay attention to your body, soul, and mind and attending to their needs.

Your body can be urging you to take a little nap, get a full-body massage, or pick up the phone and call your long-dormant relative. Write it down and carry it out on the same day.

Do You know Yourself?

How well-aware of yourself are you? Fill out a page of the autobiography below. Avoid thinking too much and just write whatever comes to mind.

Name:

Introduce Yourself

Favorites

Food:
Place:
Color:
Sport:
Animal:
Movie:
Song:
Singer:
Book:
Subject:

Hobbies

Likes

Dislikes

Day 1

_____
_____
_____
_____
_____
_____

_____
_____
_____
_____

Record the feelings you felt for listening

Day 2

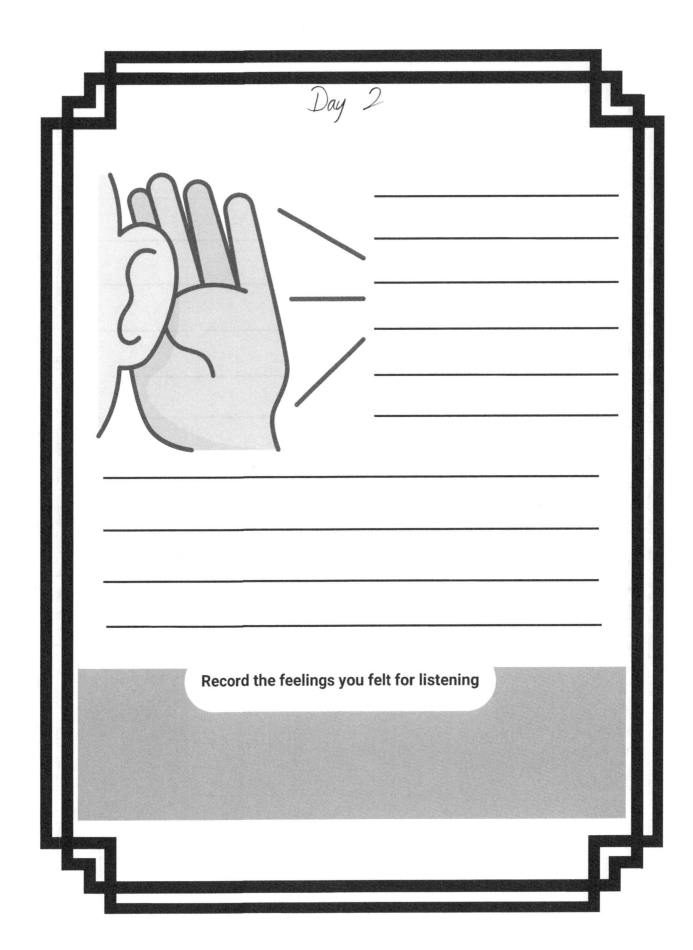

Record the feelings you felt for listening

Day 3

Record the feelings you felt for listening

Day 4

_____
_____
_____
_____
_____
_____

_____
_____
_____
_____

Record the feelings you felt for listening

Day 5

Record the feelings you felt for listening

PROMPTS

Which activities did your body demand?

Which activities did your mind and spirit demand from you?

PRANER

Dear Heavenly Father,

I come to you seeking for my true identity in you as it is written that I was created in your image. Give me the wisdom to find myself again and serve the purpose that you made me for.

In Jesus's name, Amen.

BIBLE MEDITATTION

The Bible teaches that receiving Christ's gift of everlasting life through faith includes acknowledging our identity in Him. In order to defeat death and sanctify those who believe in Him, Jesus gave His life on earth and rose from the tomb. Check out these scriptures from the Bible regarding our identity in Christ.

1 Corinthians 6:17 *- "But whoever is united with the Lord is one with him in spirit."*

Romans 6:6 *- "For we know that our old self was crucified with him so that the body ruled by sin might be done away with, that we should no longer be slaves to sin"*

SELF-ESTEEM

Ephesians 2:10 (NIV) -"For we are God's handiwork, created in Christ Jesus to do good works, which God prepared in advance for us to do."

If a partner broke up with you, it's typical for you to begin analyzing your looks and attitude and wondering what could possibly be wrong with you for someone to lose interest in you.

It might be challenging to maintain your self-esteem after splitting up with your significant other. Whatever the cause of the breakup, it may frequently make you feel less confident in yourself.

In a partnership, nobody is flawless. But assuming exclusive responsibility for the split will only cause you long-term harm.

Instead, concentrate on motivating yourself and maintaining a healthy level of self-esteem after a breakup.

When you're able to accomplish that, you'll be better equipped to deal with the loss. Additionally, it will speed up the progression of your life.

You might be filled with regrets about what you should have done differently, and probably start hearing voices in your head like "You ain't beautiful enough or you ain't strong enough," which made them break up with you, that's a lie from the devil because you are indeed unique to God and you have a divine purpose beyond a relationship.

EXERCISE

To recover and move on, you must first improve your self-esteem. The first stage is to challenge any negative ideas that may arise in your mind following a breakup.

You may do this by memorizing a passage from the bible that expresses the total opposite and applying it as a treatment to combat those unfavorable erroneous beliefs.

All you have to do is write out the scriptures from the Bible that contradict the negative notions we've constructed about what someone could think following a breakup.

Then proceed to write out your qualities and skills that you have harnessed over the years. Write them out on the shield diagram below. Remember to focus on the positives for this exercise as we all have flaws.

Finally, compose a love letter to yourself in which you express your pride in yourself and describe how you have persevered over the years to be at this very position. Do all of this while maintaining your self-esteem.

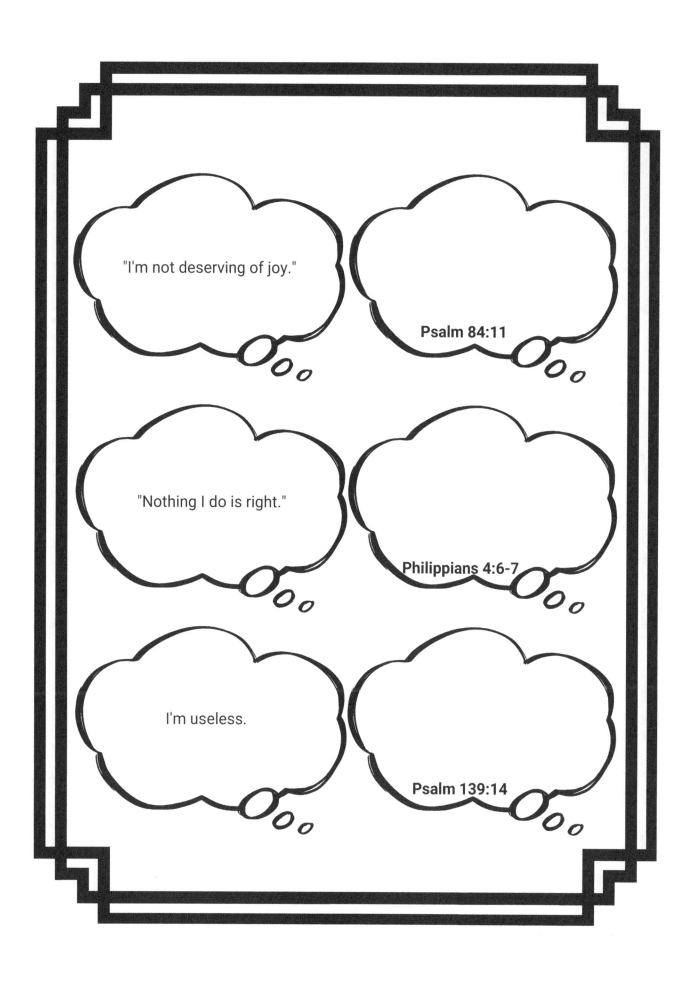

CHARACTER STRENGTHS

Choose four of your character strengths and write about them in the shield:

Dear Self,

Yours Sincerely,

_____

PROMPTS

How badly was your self-esteem affected during this breakup?

What do you think will help boost your self-esteem?

PRAYER

Dear Heavenly Father,

I come to you with all humility and seeking strength to see myself as you see. Guide me, Lord, to a place where I feel worthy of your mercy and blessings today.

In Jesus's name, Amen.

BIBLE MEDITATTION

Here are some Bible verses to help boost your self-esteem in this journey of finding yourself in Christ.

__Genesis 1:27 (NIV)__ - "So God created mankind in his own image, in the image of God he created them; male and female he created them."

__1 Corinthians 6:19-20 (NIV)__ - "Do you not know that your bodies are temples of the Holy Spirit, who is in you, whom you have received from God? You are not your own; you were bought at a price. Therefore, honor God with your bodies."

8 SOLO GOALS

Proverbs 16:3 (NIV) - *"Commit to the Lord whatever you do, and he will establish your plans."*

Everyone is aware of how tough breakups are, yet starting to create goals might help you move on.

Setting goals encourages you to make changes in your life, which is therapeutic.

Always make sure that your goals are SMART. Specific, Measurable, Actionable, Reasonable, and Timely are the letters in the acronym. A goal must be well-defined and quantifiable. Otherwise, it is only a fantasy and not a goal.

Allow yourself to reflect on your goals. Choose objectives that you truly desire rather than those you "think" you ought to have.

What you genuinely desire will draw you and give you greater drive to get it. The best part is that if you pursue the things you truly want rather than the ones you "should" desire, you'll probably achieve much more than you anticipated.

In order to achieve your goals, which are in line with God's plan for your life, you should ask for his assistance. I also want you to know that God is the only one who truly comprehends you.

A split, in my opinion, might present a chance for development and learning. This concept has assisted many of us in giving endings purpose.

Your objectives can be to earn a new degree, work on your communication abilities, or spend more time with God to hear what he has to say at this time.

Getting closer to God and discovering his plan for my life was my breakup goal, and he assisted me in achieving that. I now have a stronger spiritual life and a profound awareness of his generosity and love.

EXERCISE

Pray fervently, reflect, and think clearly before you set your goals. You do not have to rush this exercise, you can take days in prayers searching yourself as well as asking God for guidance.

Remember your goals have to be S.M.A.R.T., it demands your desire, hunger, and tenacity for it to become a reality. It won't be easy I must remind you but knowing you have the God who can do everything with you on this journey is enough to assure you of certain victory.

Use the goal-setting template below to set whatever goals you have agreed in your spirit to go after.

Make your goals...

SMART

S — Specific
What do you want to achieve?

M — Measurable
How will you track your progress?

A — Attainable
How can you reach your goal?

R — Relevant
Why is this goal important?

T — Timely
When will the goal be accomplished?

Make your goals...

S M A R T

S — Specific

What do you want to achieve?

M — **Measurable**

How will you track your progress?

A — Attainable

How can you reach your goal?

R — Relevant

Why is this goal important?

T — Timely

When will the goal be accomplished?

Make your goals...

SMART

S Specific → What do you want to achieve?

M Measurable → How will you track your progress?

A Attainable → How can you reach your goal?

R Relevant → Why is this goal important?

T Timely → When will the goal be accomplished?

Make your goals...

SMART

S Specific → What do you want to achieve?

M Measurable → How will you track your progress?

A Attainable → How can you reach your goal?

R Relevant → Why is this goal important?

T Timely → When will the goal be accomplished?

PROMPTS

Why did you pick these goals to pursue?

What difficulty do you expect to face in chasing these goals?

PRAYER

Dear Heavenly Father,

My God, my creator, thank you for your love and guidance in this season, I ask that you help me achieve these goals as they are important to me and I pray that I reach the purpose that you've set me out for.

In Jesus's name, Amen.

BIBLE MEDITATTION

Meditate on these Bible verses as you set out to achieve these goals knowing that the All-knowing God is there with you at all times.

Philippians 3:14 (NIV) *- "I press on toward the goal to win the prize for which God has called me heavenward in Christ Jesus."*

Proverbs 21:5 (NIV) *- "The plans of the diligent lead to profit as surely as haste leads to poverty."*

9 SUPPORT CIRCLE

Proverbs 15:22 (NIV): "Plans fail for lack of counsel, but with many advisers, they succeed."

It makes sense that following a breakup, you would want to rely on your friends for comfort. Be careful not to allow fear of seeming foolish or humiliation to prevent you from pursuing that action.

Find individuals in your life who will listen to you and even be accommodating when you need to express your unhappiness with the relationship. Avoid believing that you don't want to be a burden to anyone right now.

Remember *Ecclesiastes 4:9-10 (NIV): "Two are better than one because they have a good return for their labor: If either of them falls down, one can help the other up. But pity anyone who falls and has no one to help them up."*

Don't spend the entire day feeling down or depressed; instead, schedule a dinner date with friends and family and try that new restaurant. Be joyful and trust in the Lord; everything happens for a purpose. Whatever you pick, just be with people you love and trust.

Be open and honest with those you've chosen to spend time with; do not keep your feelings hidden. You need them now more than ever because you can't accomplish this on your own.

When my relationship ended, I recall reestablishing contact with several old college friends who assisted me in moving on more quickly than I had anticipated.

Do not feel ashamed about this situation; practically everyone has breakups. When I opened up about my breakup, they all shared stories of their own breakups, which helped me recover even more quickly.

Do not disregard what the creator has given you since God has provided us with other people to assist us. Just as they are there for you now, so will you be for them later on in their need.

EXERCISE

Keep in mind that you are not alone on this road to healing and recovery; there are many people out there who are willing to hear your story and support you. I had a lot of support from my family during my personal split.

Don't ignore these groups of individuals; the support and counsel I got from each and every one of them helped me advance quickly. There is a trust circle below. Consider who you know you can trust, write their names inside the circle, reach out to them, and let them know what has happened.

Be truthful about how and why this relationship ended. As Christians, you shouldn't try to discredit your ex-partner. Say fully what happened, signal the end, and incline toward solace.

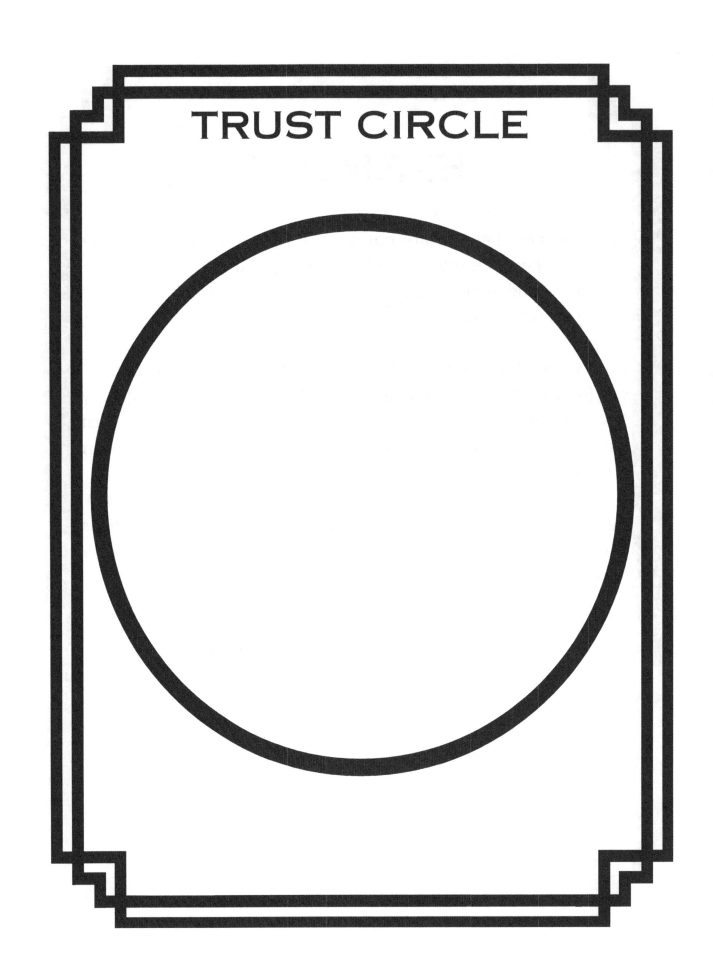

TRUST CIRCLE

PROMPTS

How do you feel about opening up to others?

What exactly do you need from your support circle right now?

PRAYER

Dear Heavenly Father,

My God, grant me the freedom to clearly express the grief in my heart to those around me. Take away any pride that will stop me from being honest about my pain.

In Jesus's name, Amen.

BIBLE MEDITATTION

These Bible verses are to encourage you to let others help you in your hour of need. God created them to be your support.

1 Thessalonians 5:11 (NIV) - *"Therefore encourage one another and build each other up, just as in fact you are doing."*

Proverbs 19:20 (NIV) - *"Listen to advice and accept discipline, and at the end, you will be counted among the wise."*

PATIENCE

Being patient might be one of the most difficult fruits of the spirit to develop, yet a patient Christian is smart. Waiting for God and others is challenging. Both your mending and entering your next relationship should take time. Give yourself time to recover properly.

I understand that you might miss the late-night calls, having someone to talk to about your day, and perhaps a dinner date, but I will still advise you to be patient and avoid trying to rebound from a broken relationship because most people who do so tend to regret their decision.

All wounds mend with time. Date yourself for the time being as you recuperate. By concentrating on developing mentally, physically, spiritually, and financially

If you learn that your ex-partner is now in a relationship, you might feel motivated to move on quickly. However, moving on is not a competition. You don't need to convince anyone of anything. You are much desired by God and He loves you.

Pray and be ready to hear from God. Most times we get into a relationship without seeking wisdom from God first, God still speaks to us as humans, and we are no different. Involve God in everything even the things you consider tiny.

It is written in **Romans 12:12 (NIV) - *"Be joyful in hope, patient in affliction, faithful in prayer."*** God will never abandon nor forsake even in this new season as long as you prioritize him, be patient with God and you will see his mighty hand in everything.

EXERCISE

Congratulations!!! You have come this far and I do hope you're healing as expected. God cares about everything that concerns us but we must be patient to see his hand in these things, especially in our relationships.

No one is flawless, but there are some basic traits you need in your next partner. Take your time to state those qualities, pray to God about it, and wait patiently.

Use the illustration below, to state these qualities out and know that God is thinking about you as well.

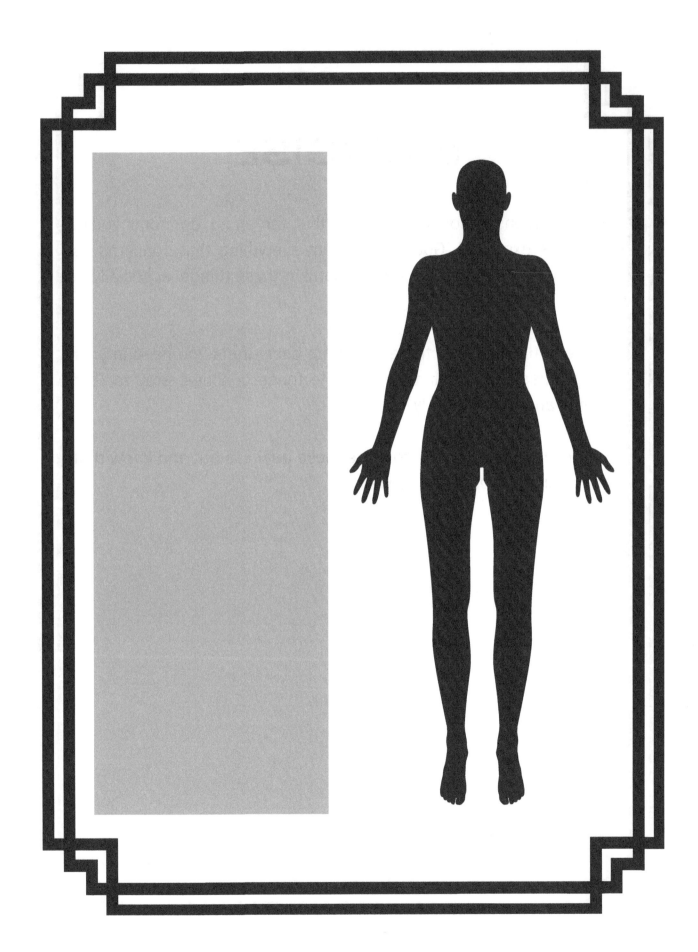

PROMPTS

What do you need most from your next partner?

_____

_____

What do you feel your next partner will enjoy most from you?

_____

_____

_____

PRAYER

Dear Heavenly Father,

My God, grant me the spirit of patience to wait on you Lord for my healing and my next relationship. Teach me to pray and be closer to you even while in love.

In Jesus's name, Amen.

BIBLE MEDITATTION

These verses will encourage you to trust God and be patient to wait for him for his divine healing and direction.

James 5:7-8 (NIV) *- "Be patient, then, brothers and sisters, until the Lord's coming. See how the farmer waits for the land to yield its valuable crop, patiently waiting for the autumn and spring rains. You too, be patient and stand firm, because the Lord's coming is near."*

Ephesians 4:2 (NIV) *- "Be completely humble and gentle; be patient, bearing with one another in love."*

Made in the USA
Middletown, DE
03 June 2025